Compromising Positions

Ladies in Red

By Anita Cocktail

Compromising Positions

GORGEOUS GIRLS IN RED LINGERIE

Copyright © Compromising Positions 2015

Compiled By Anita Cocktail

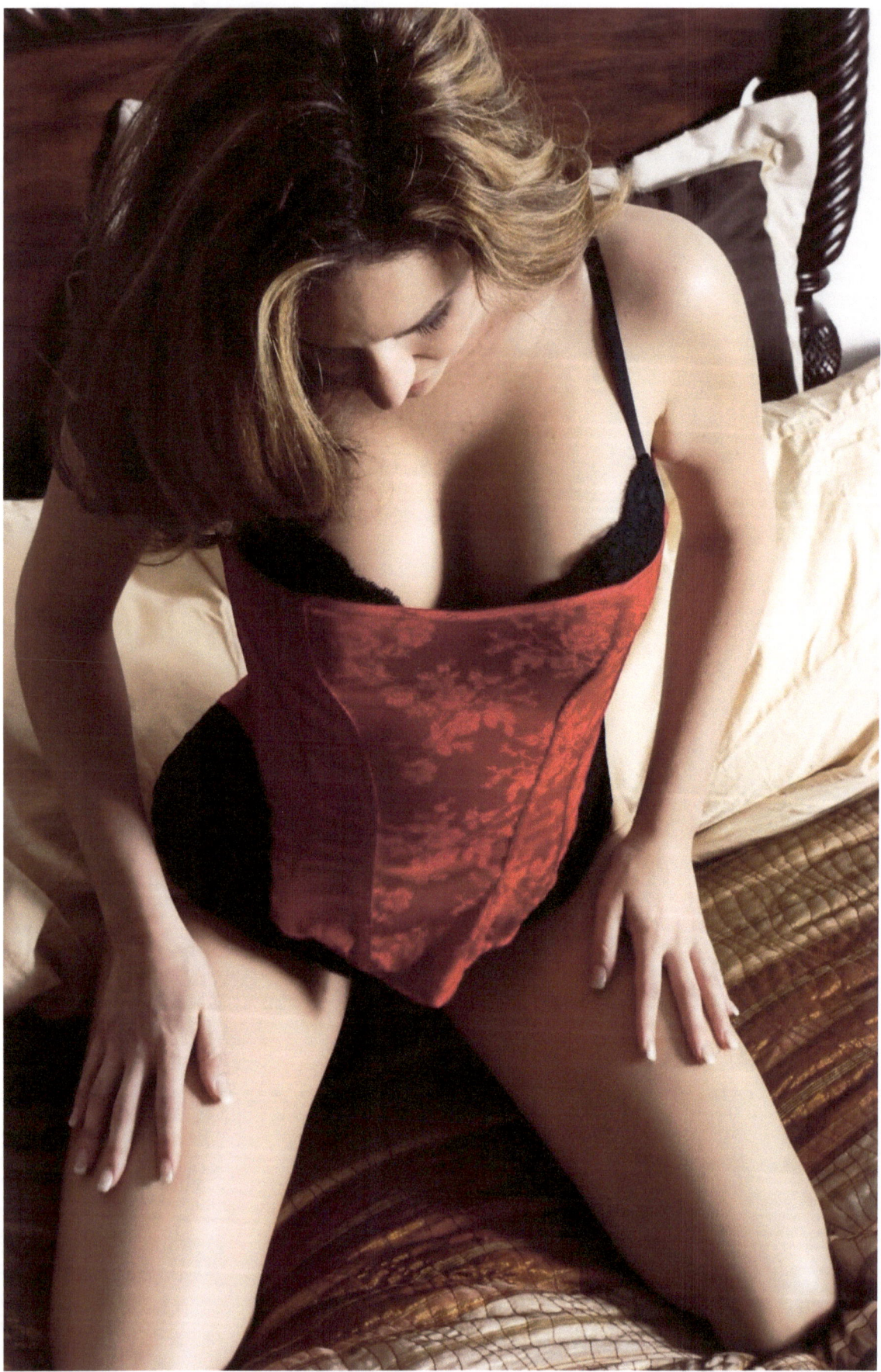

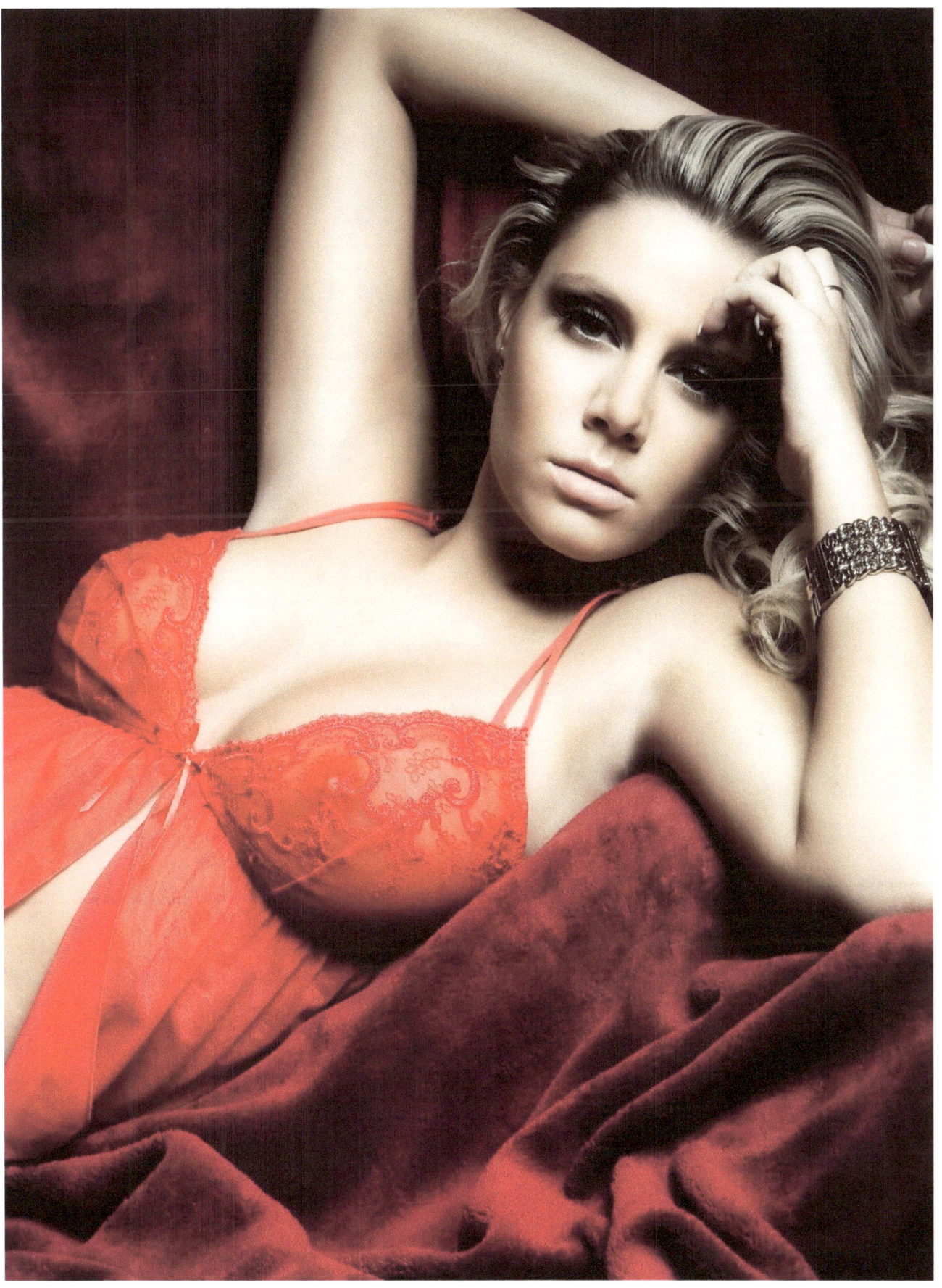

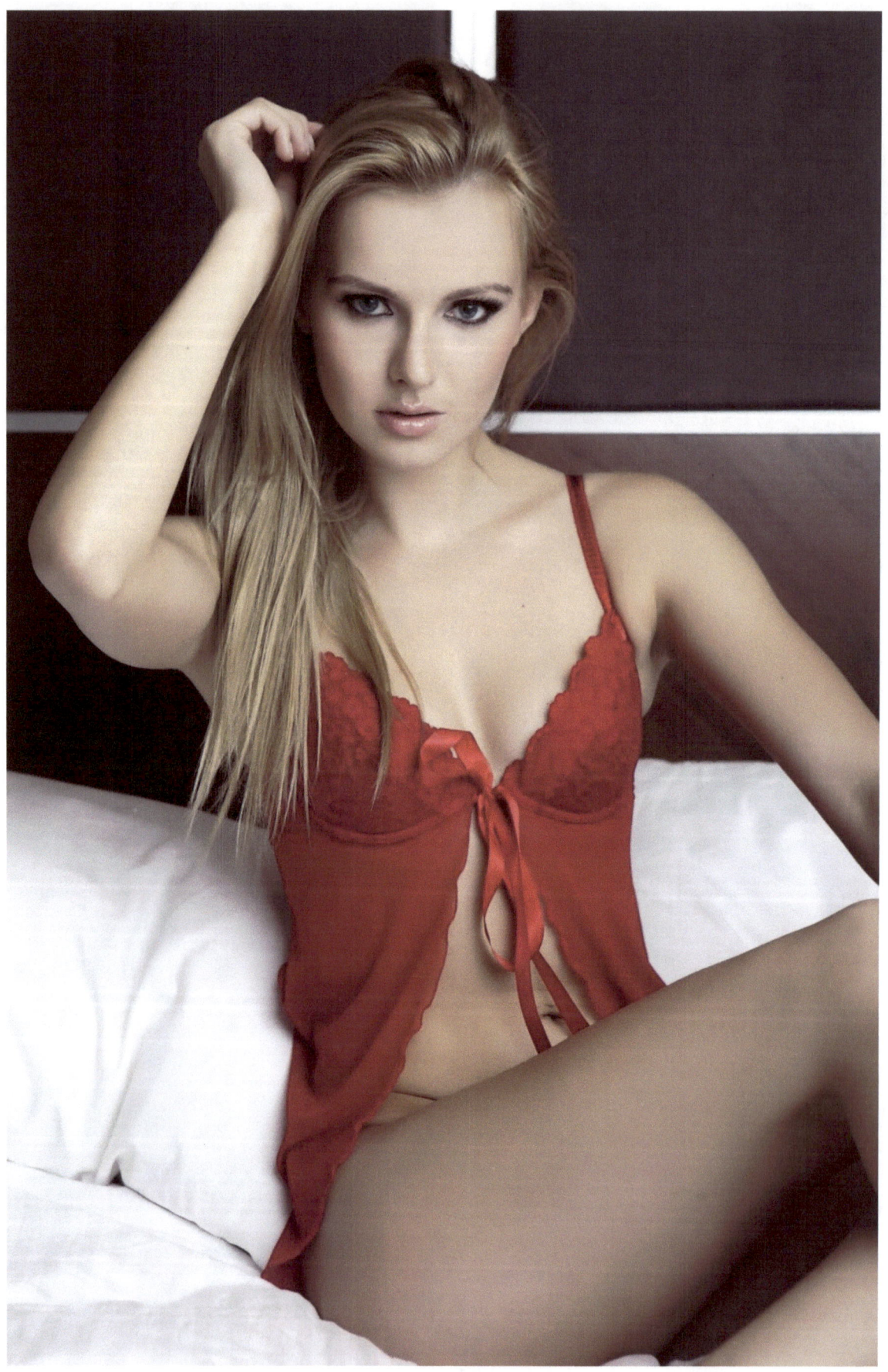

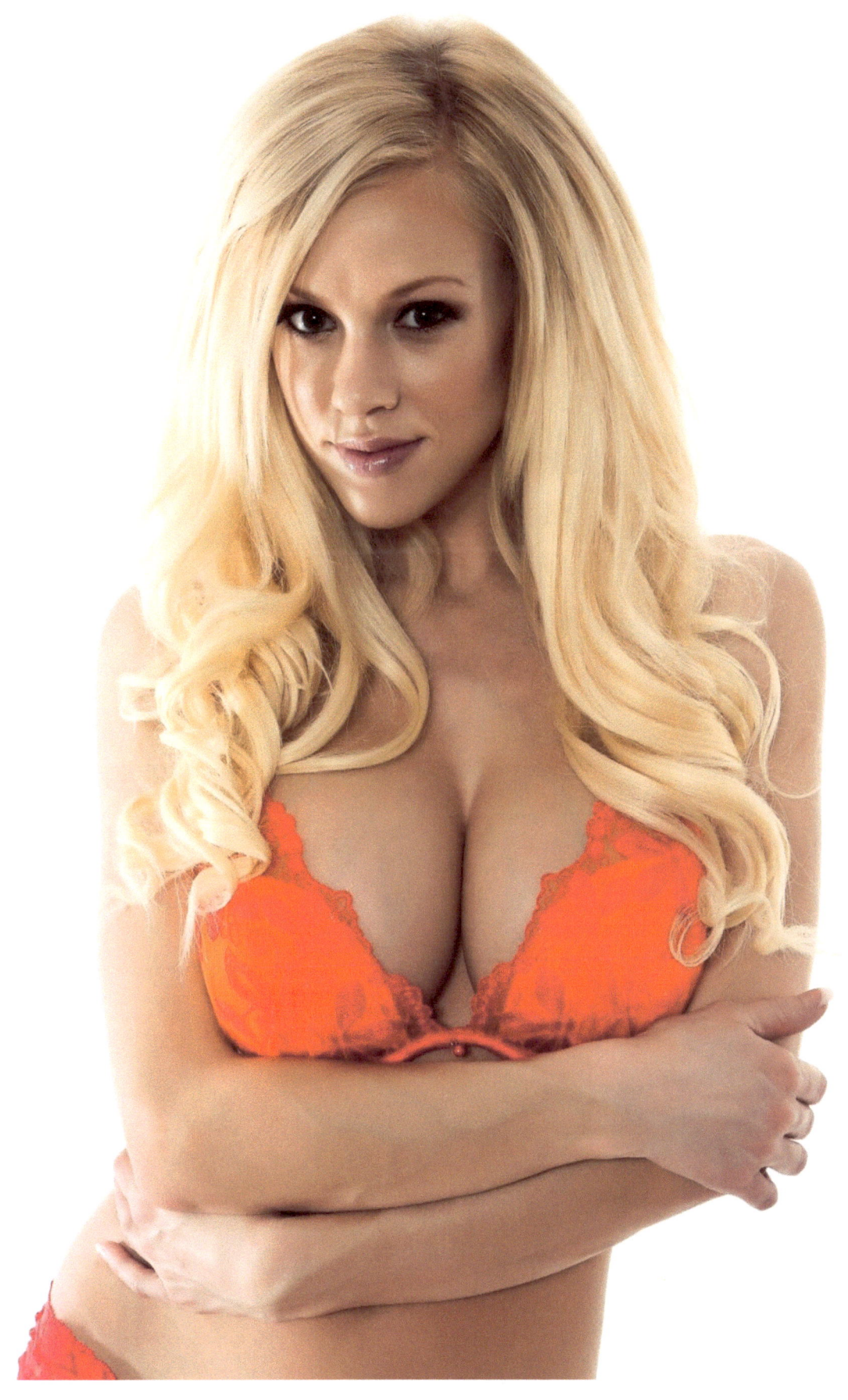

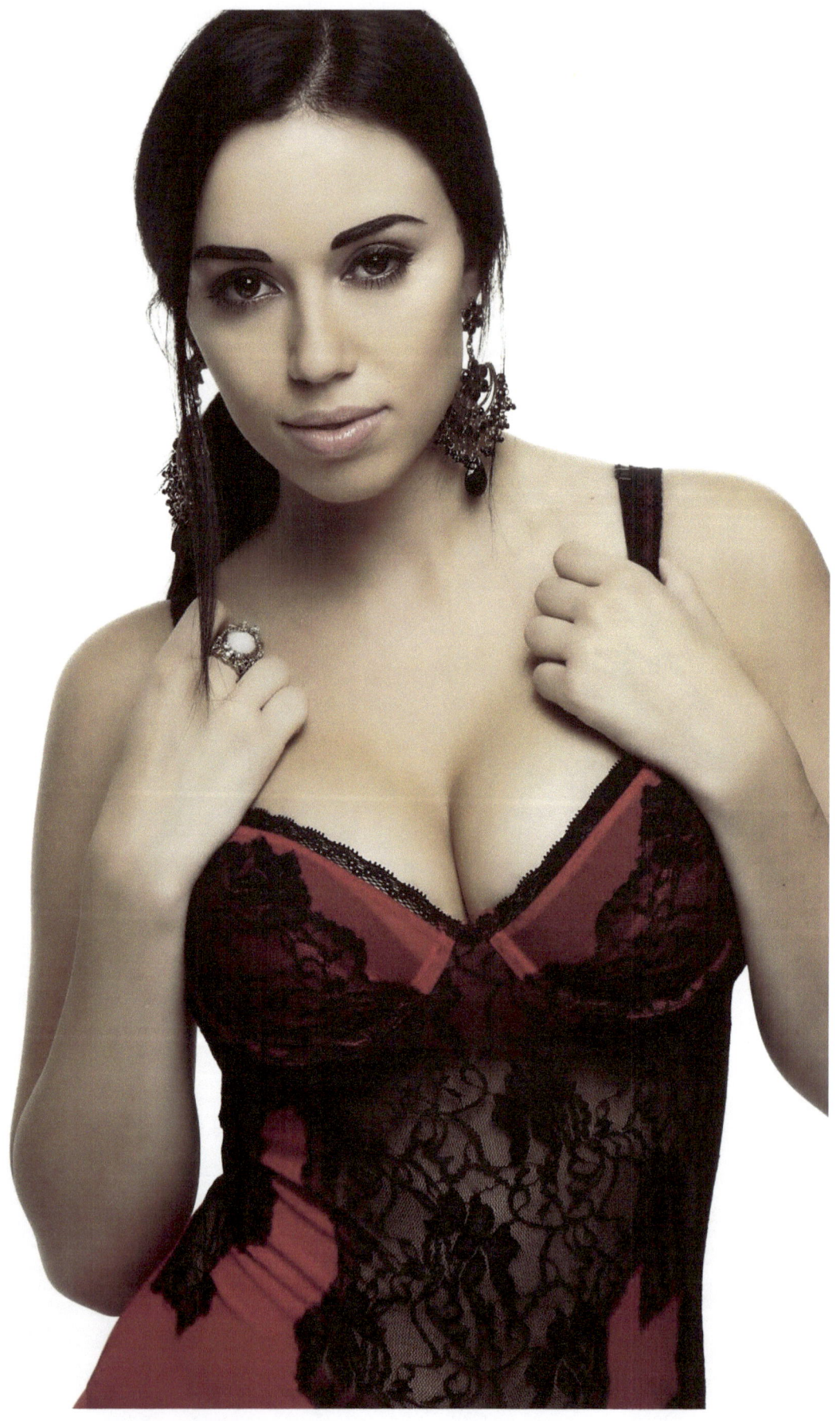

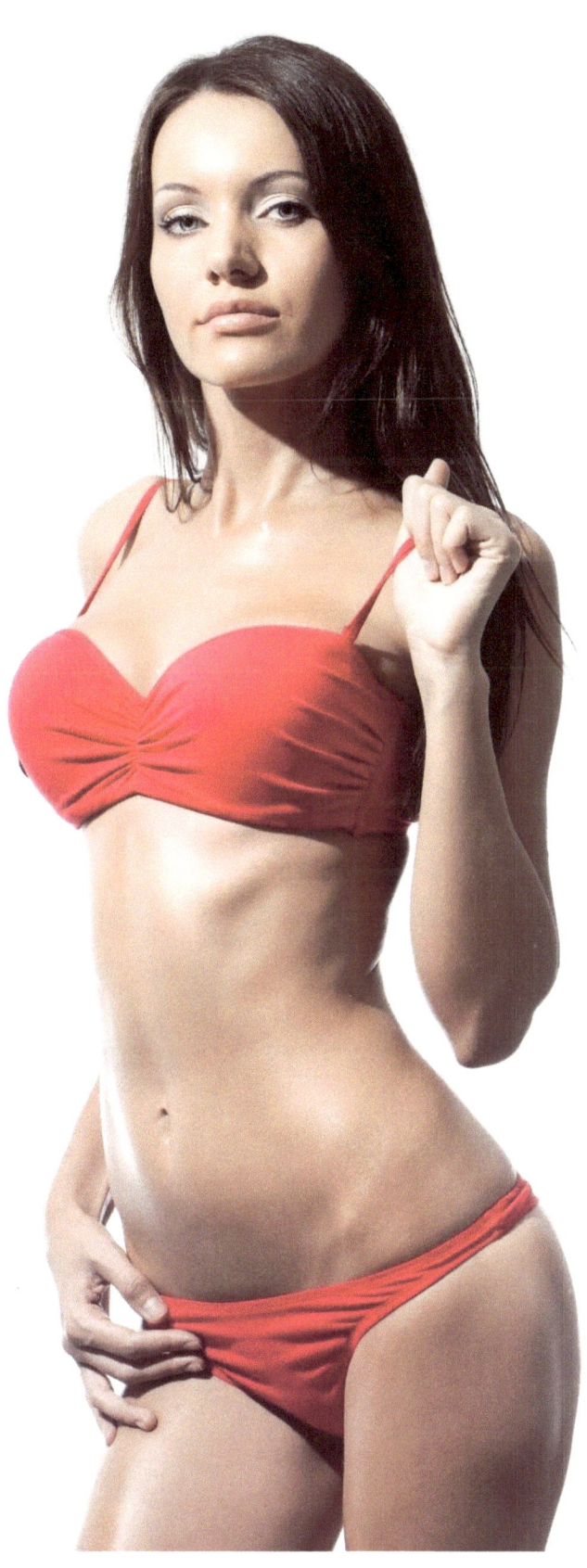

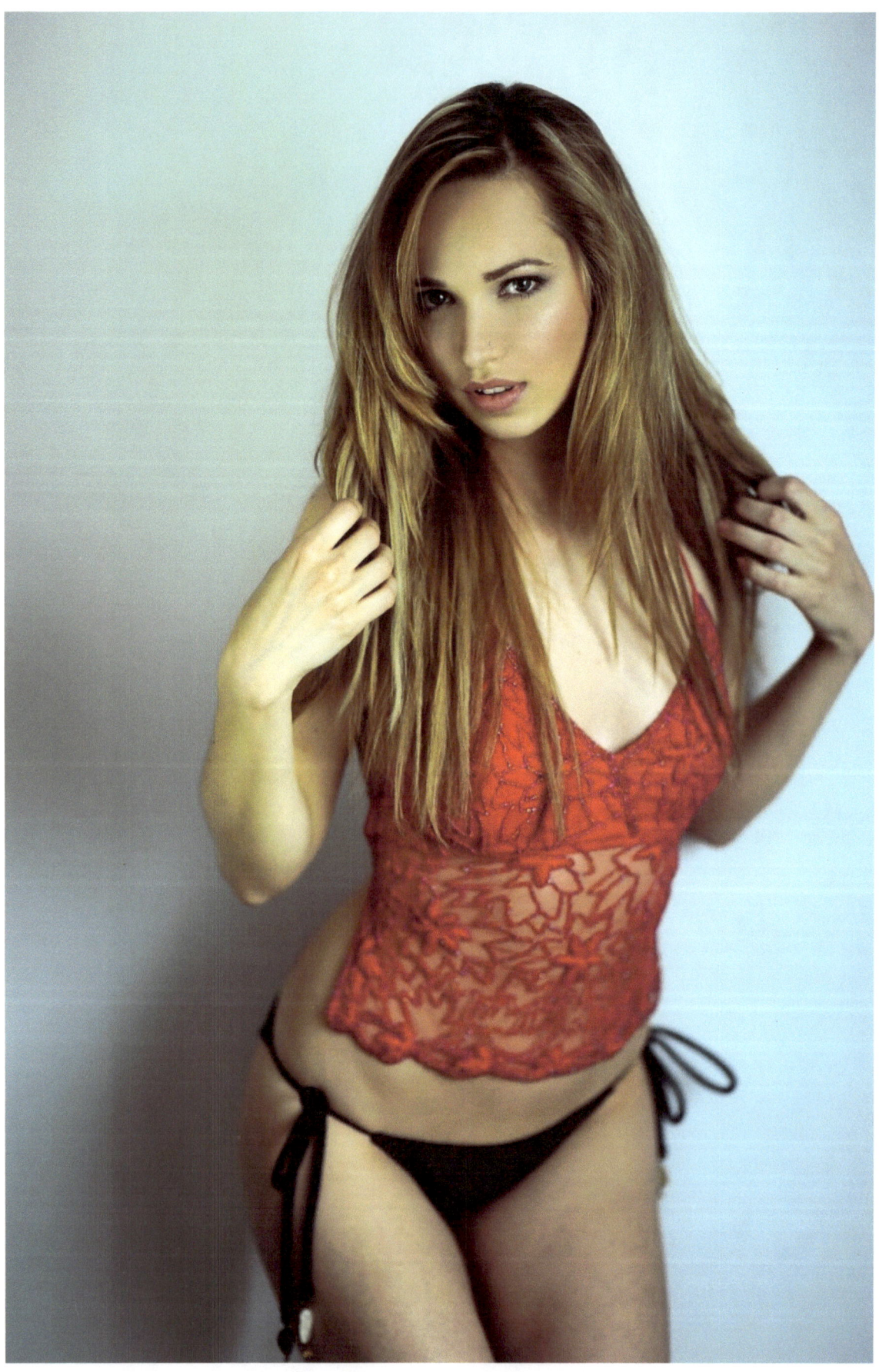

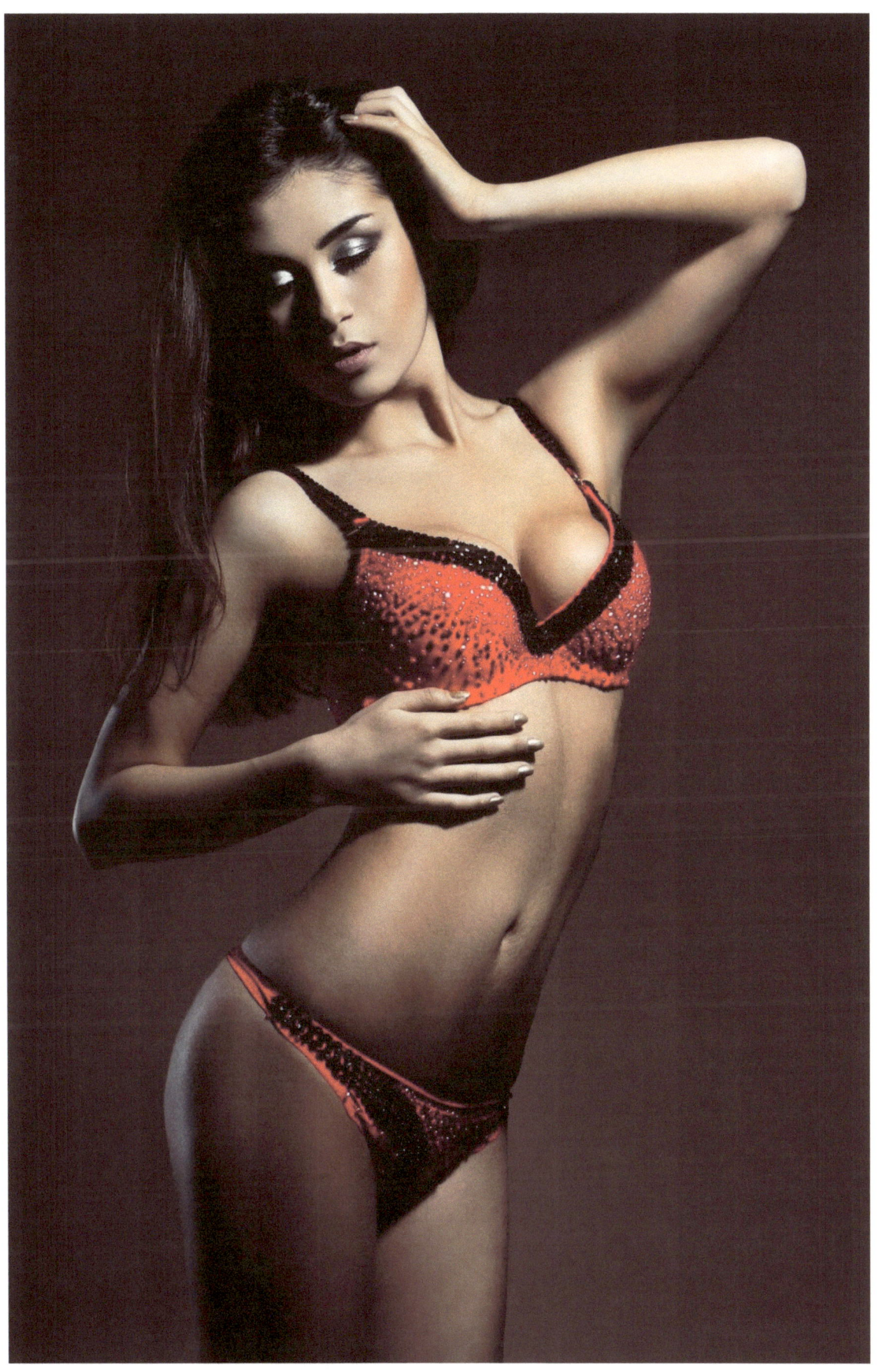

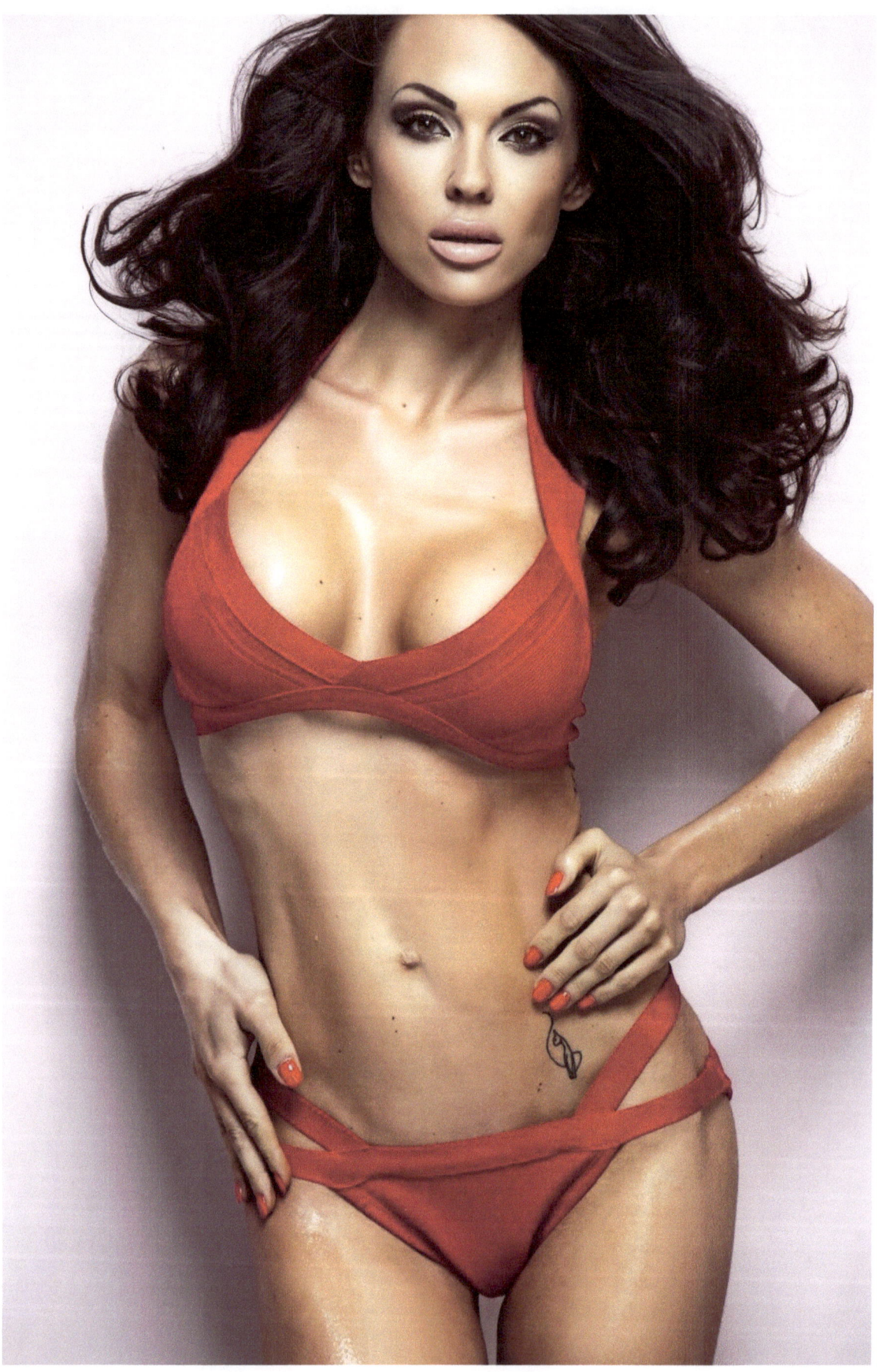

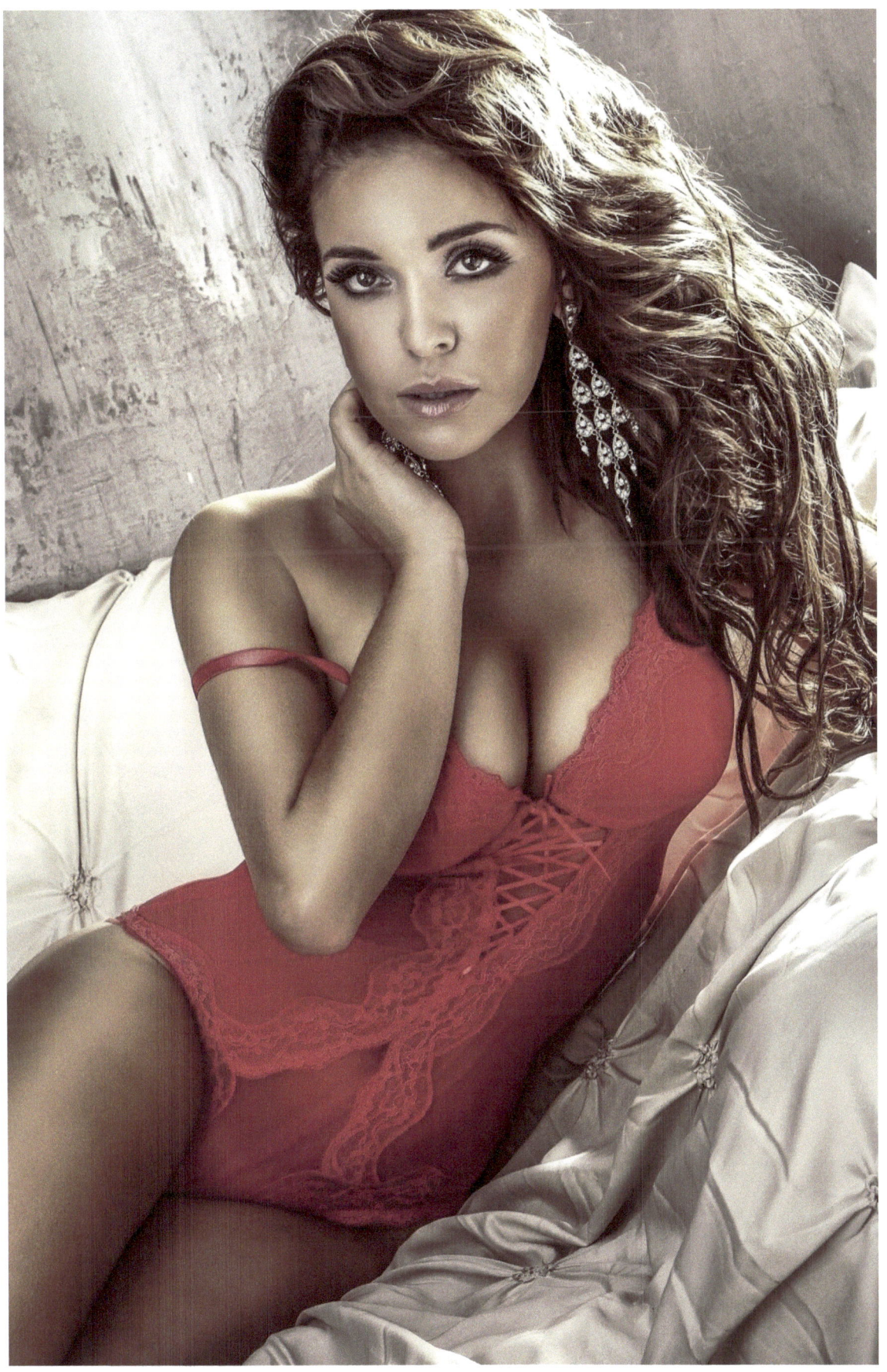

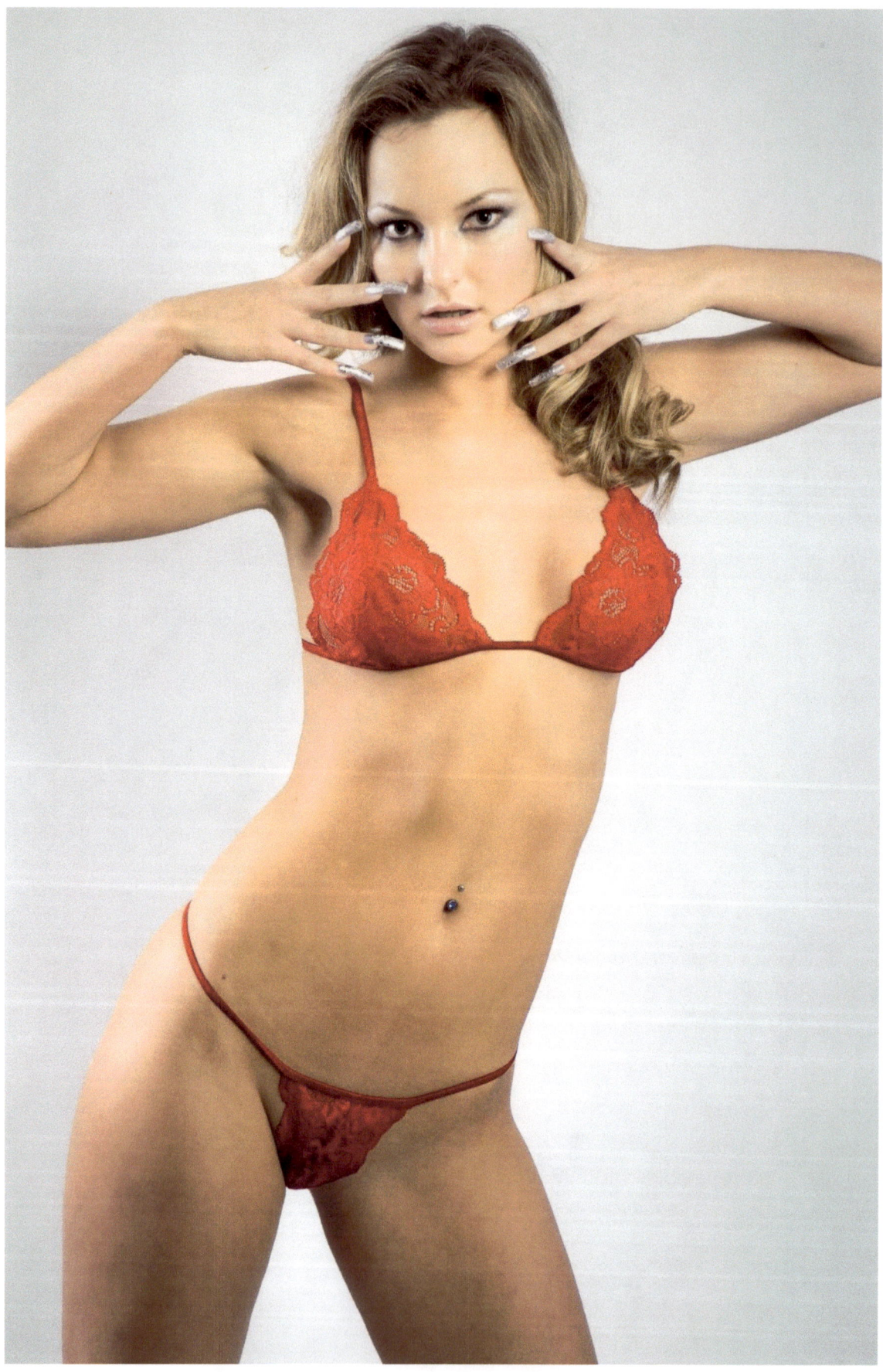

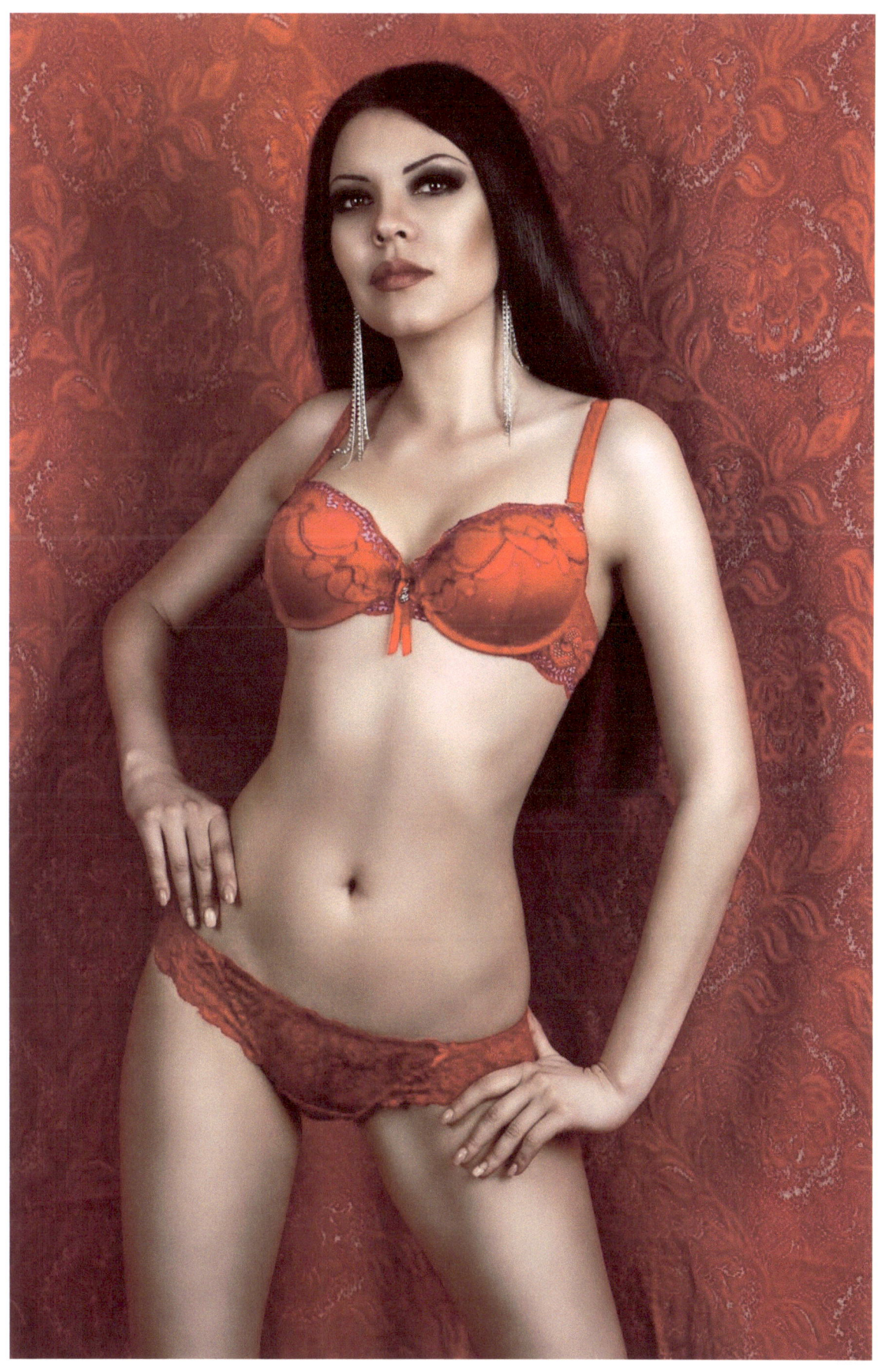

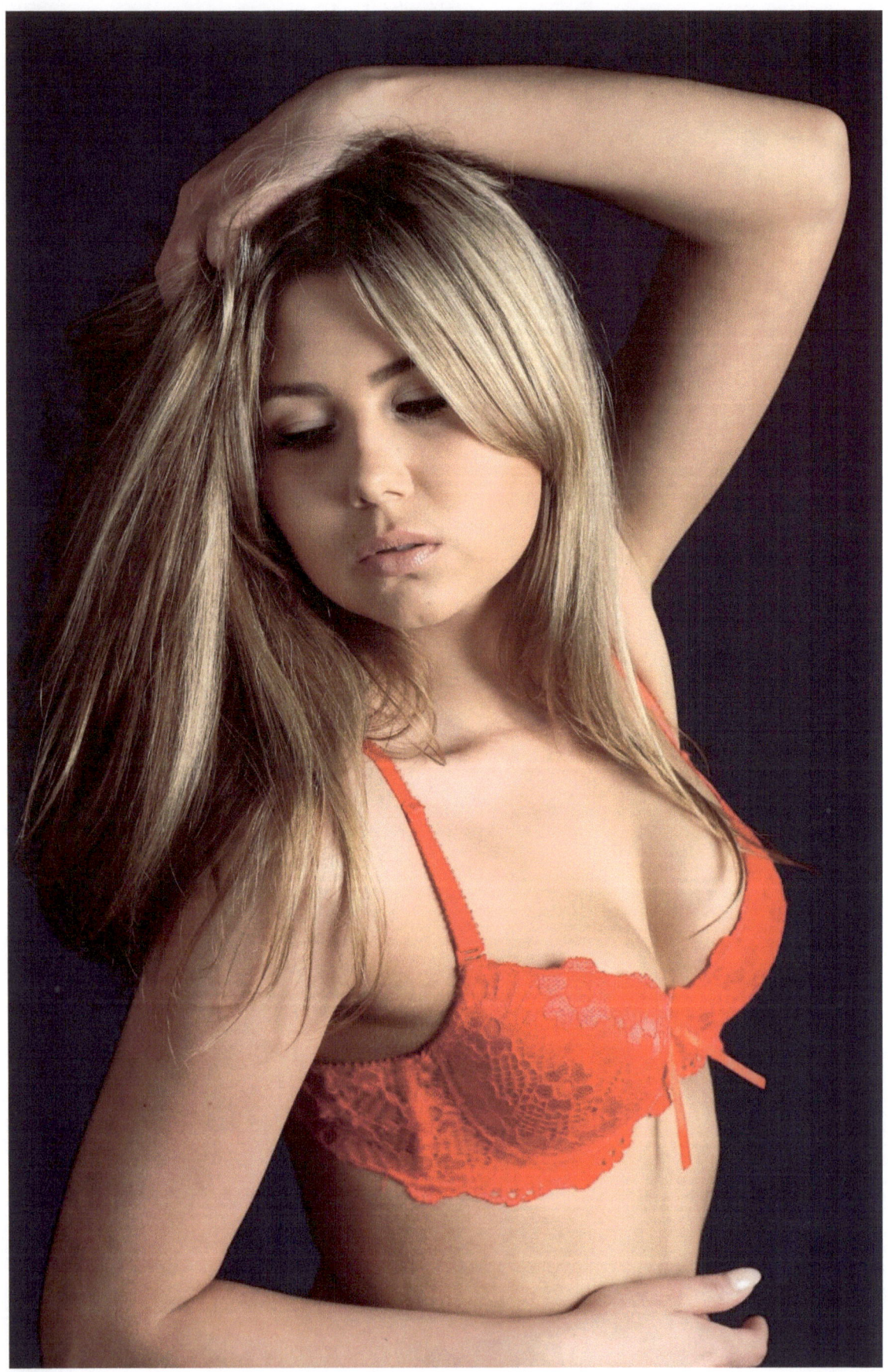

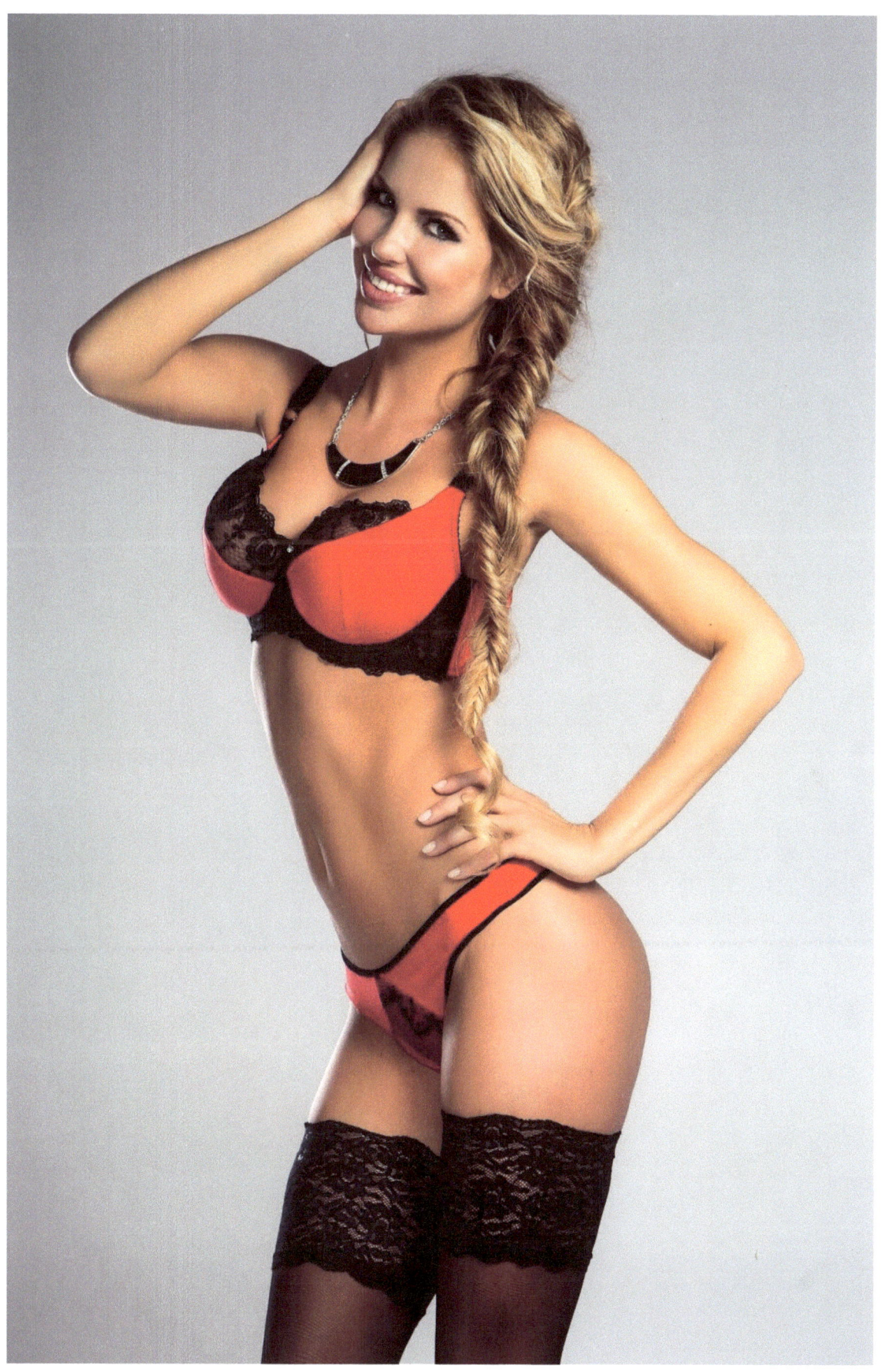

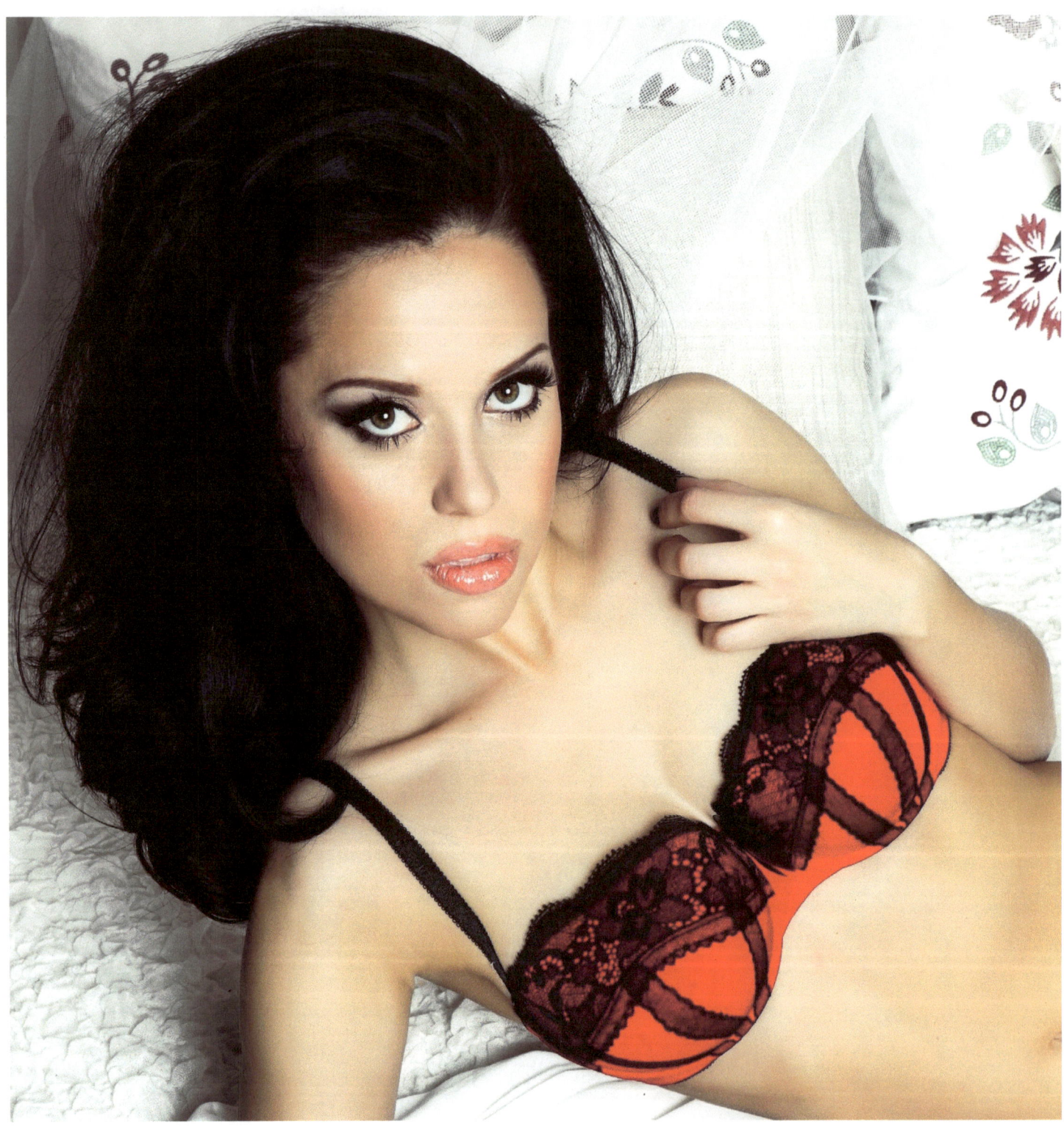

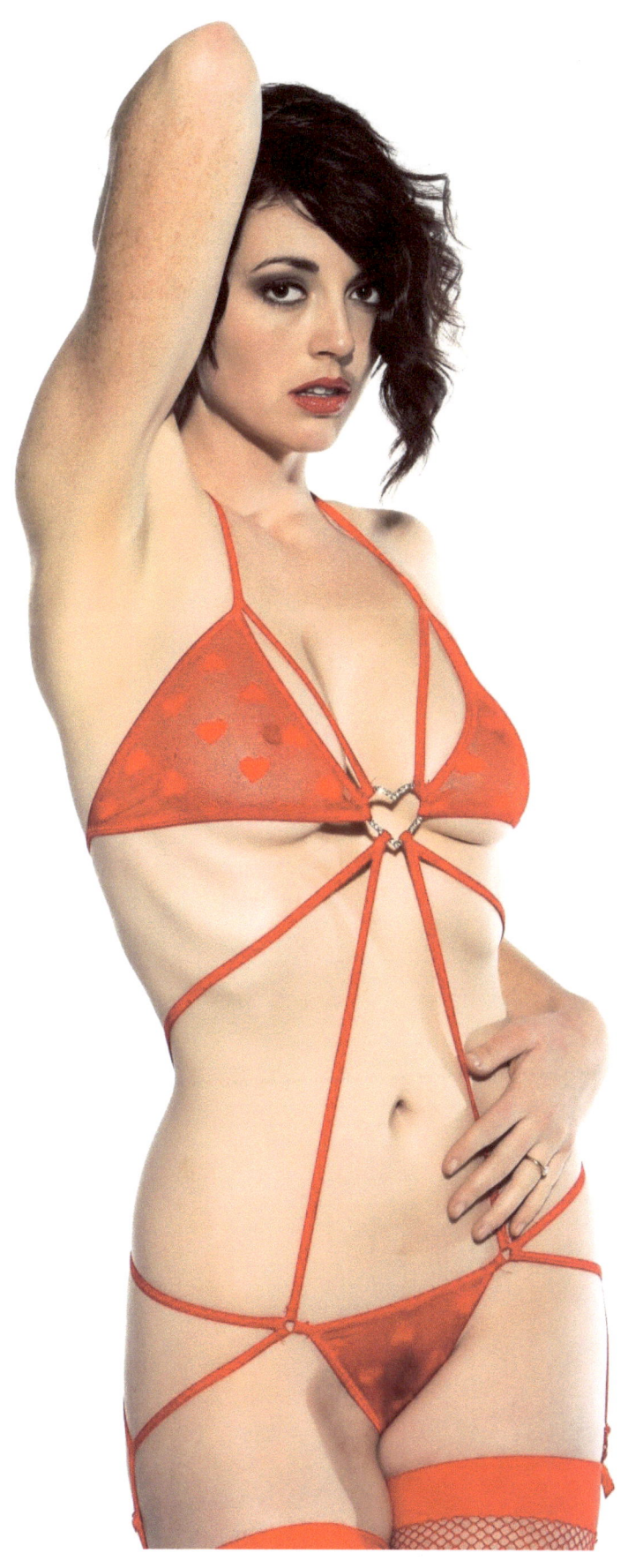

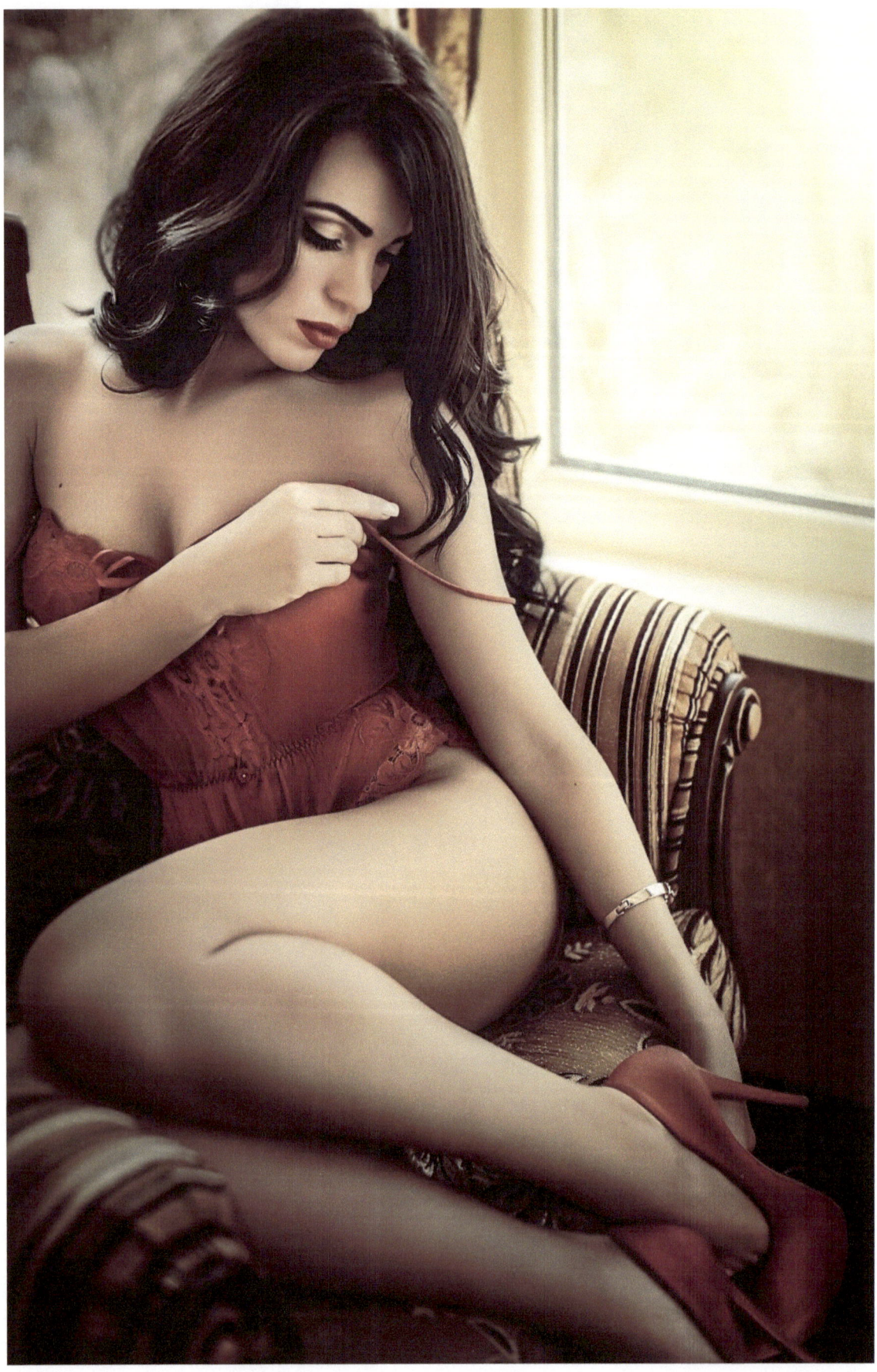

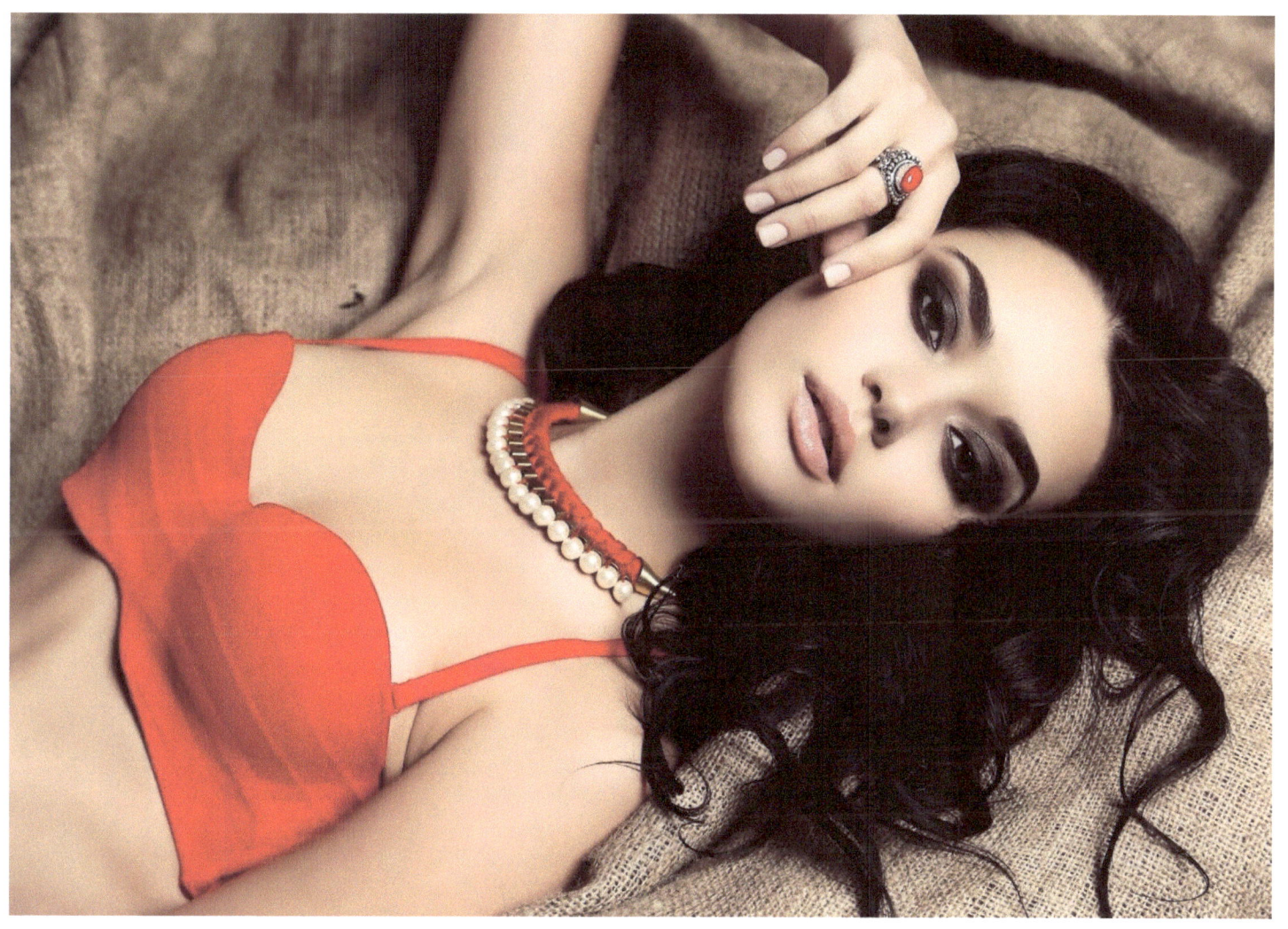

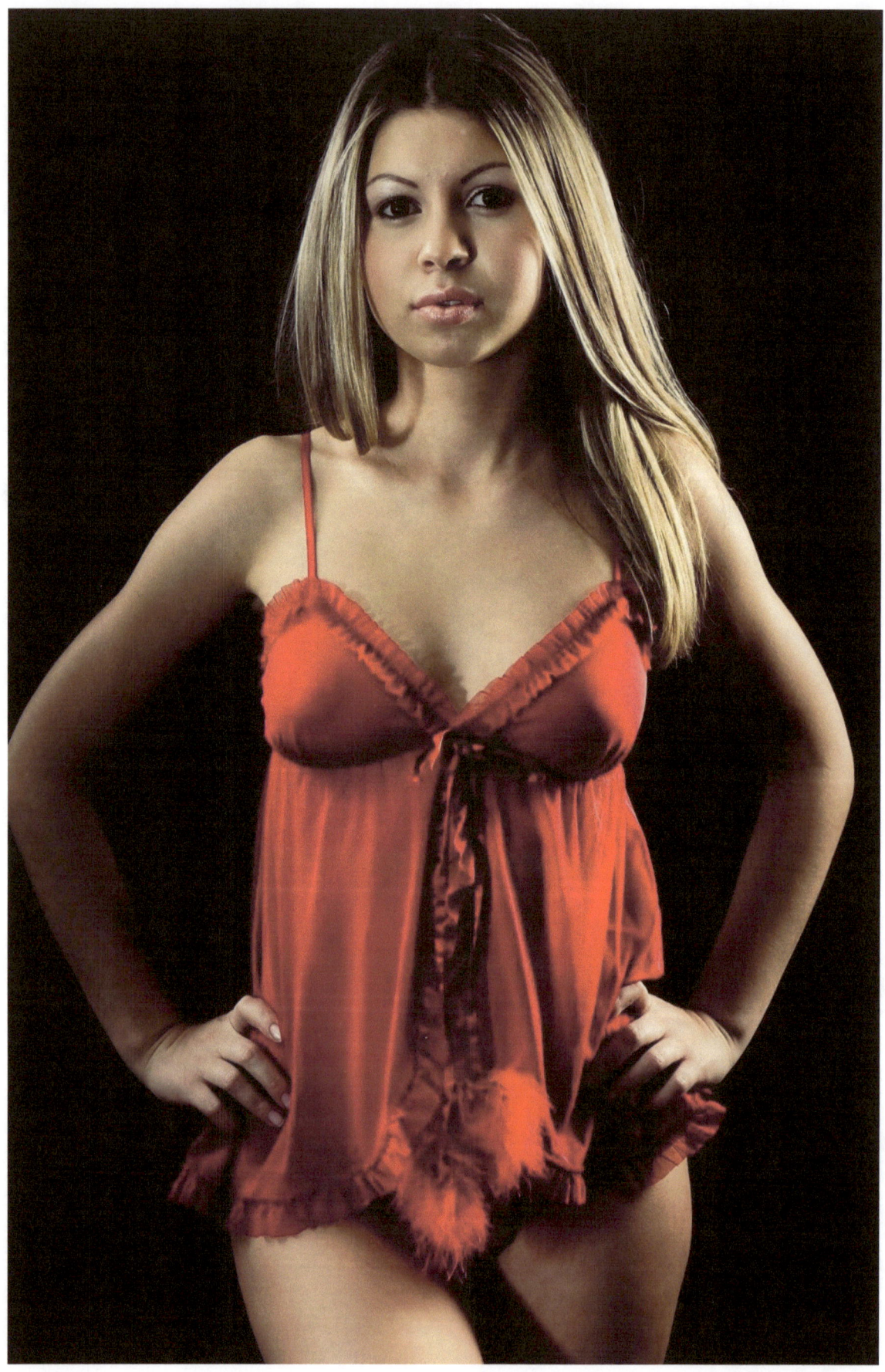

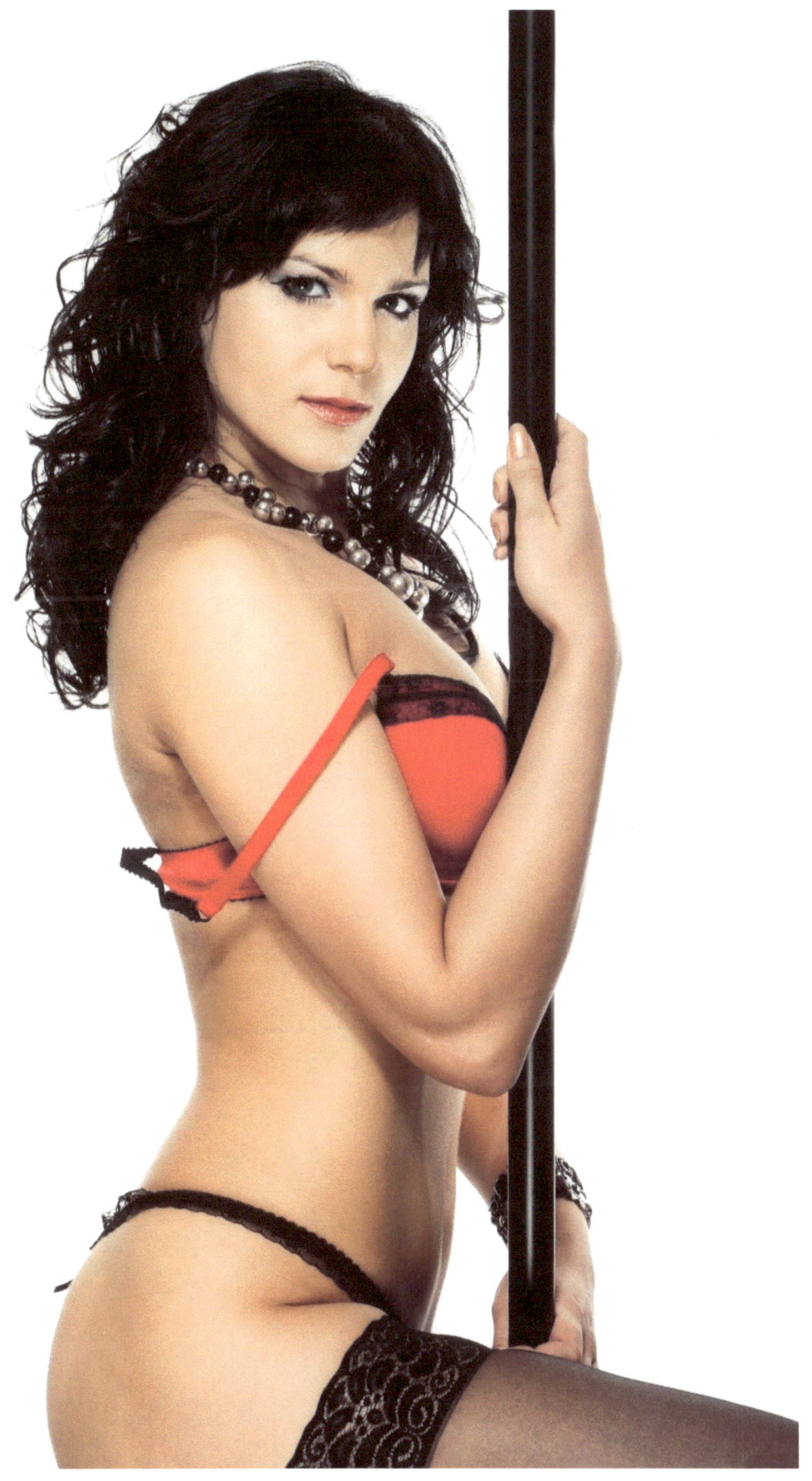

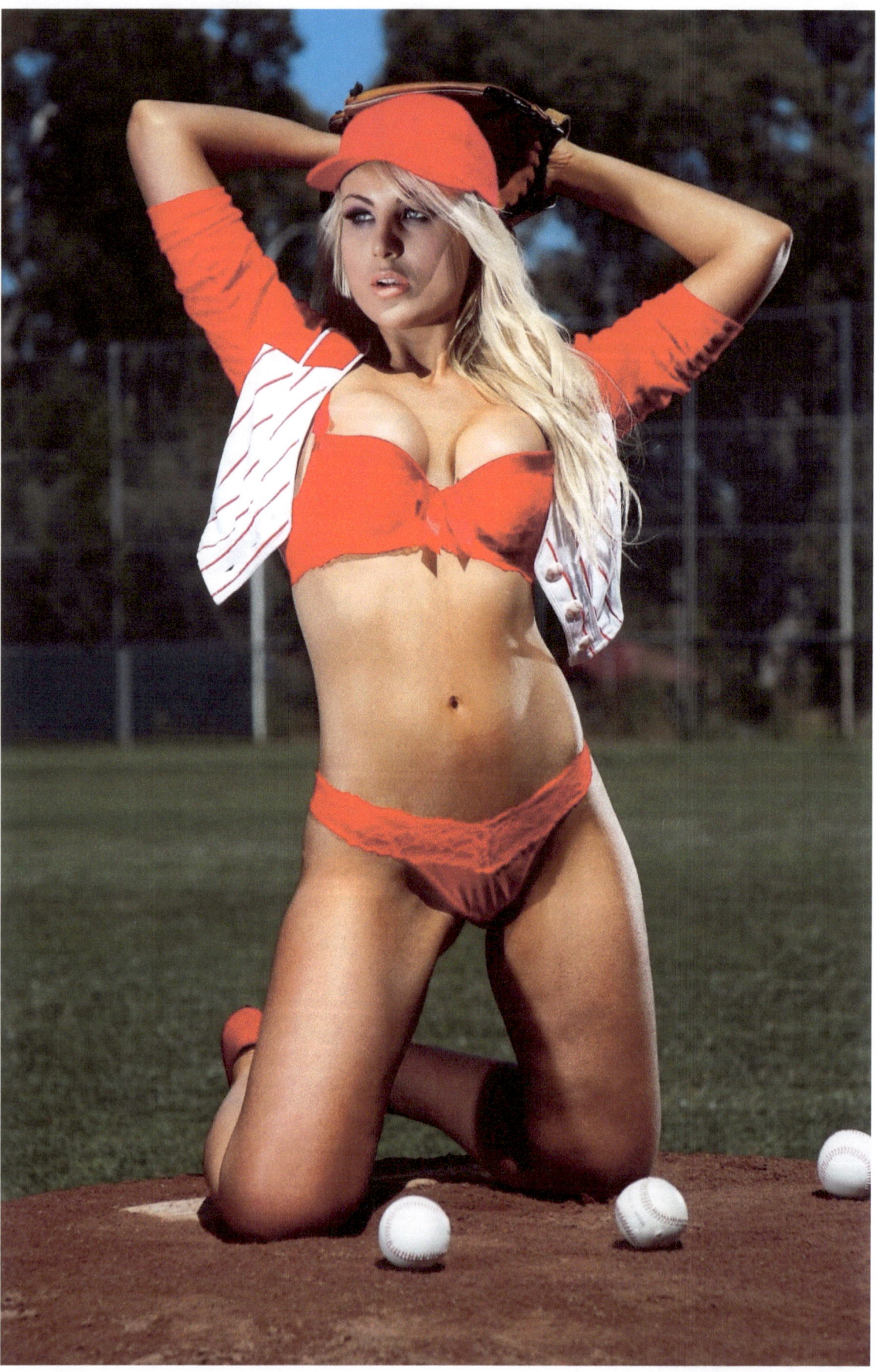

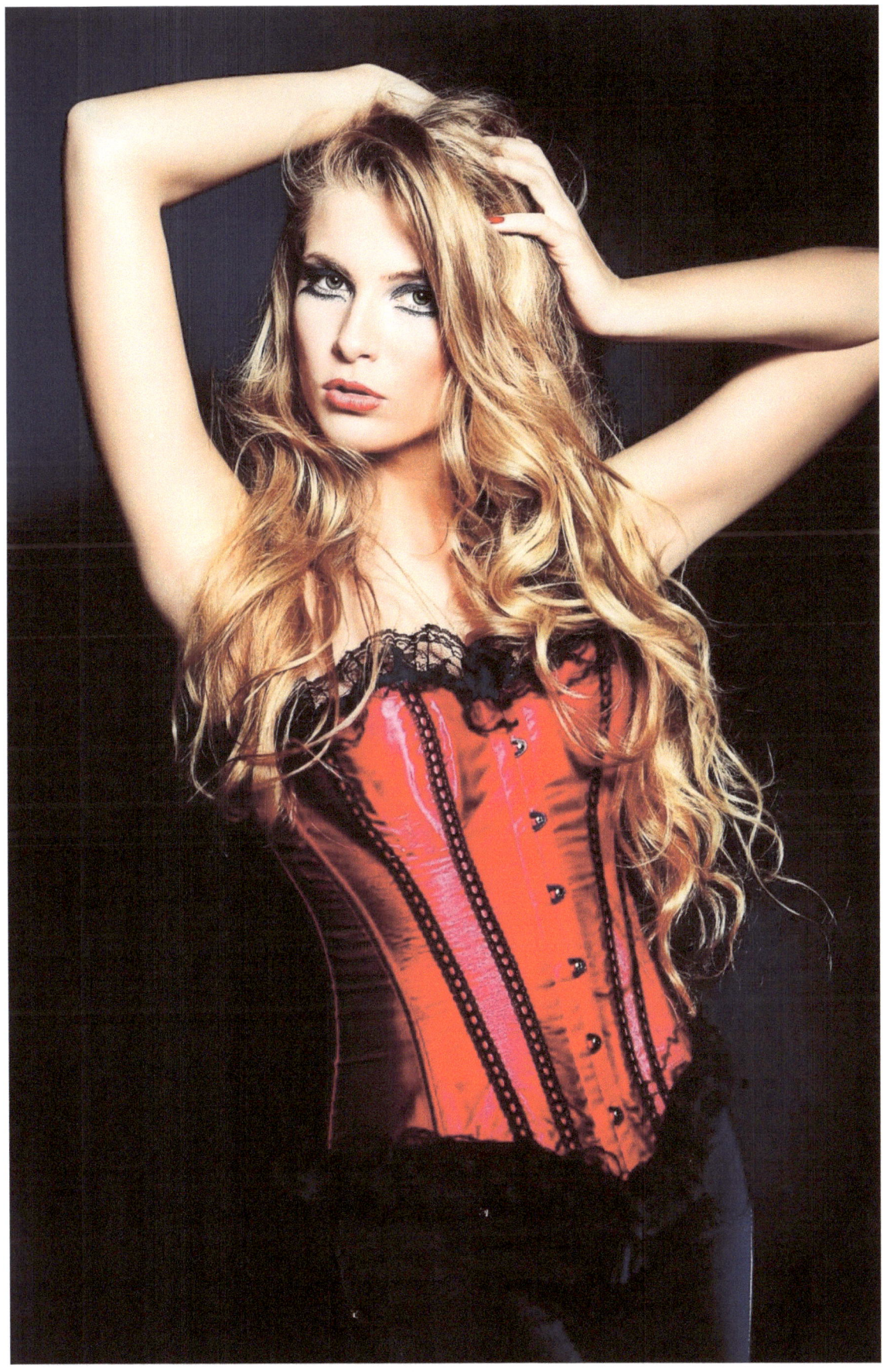

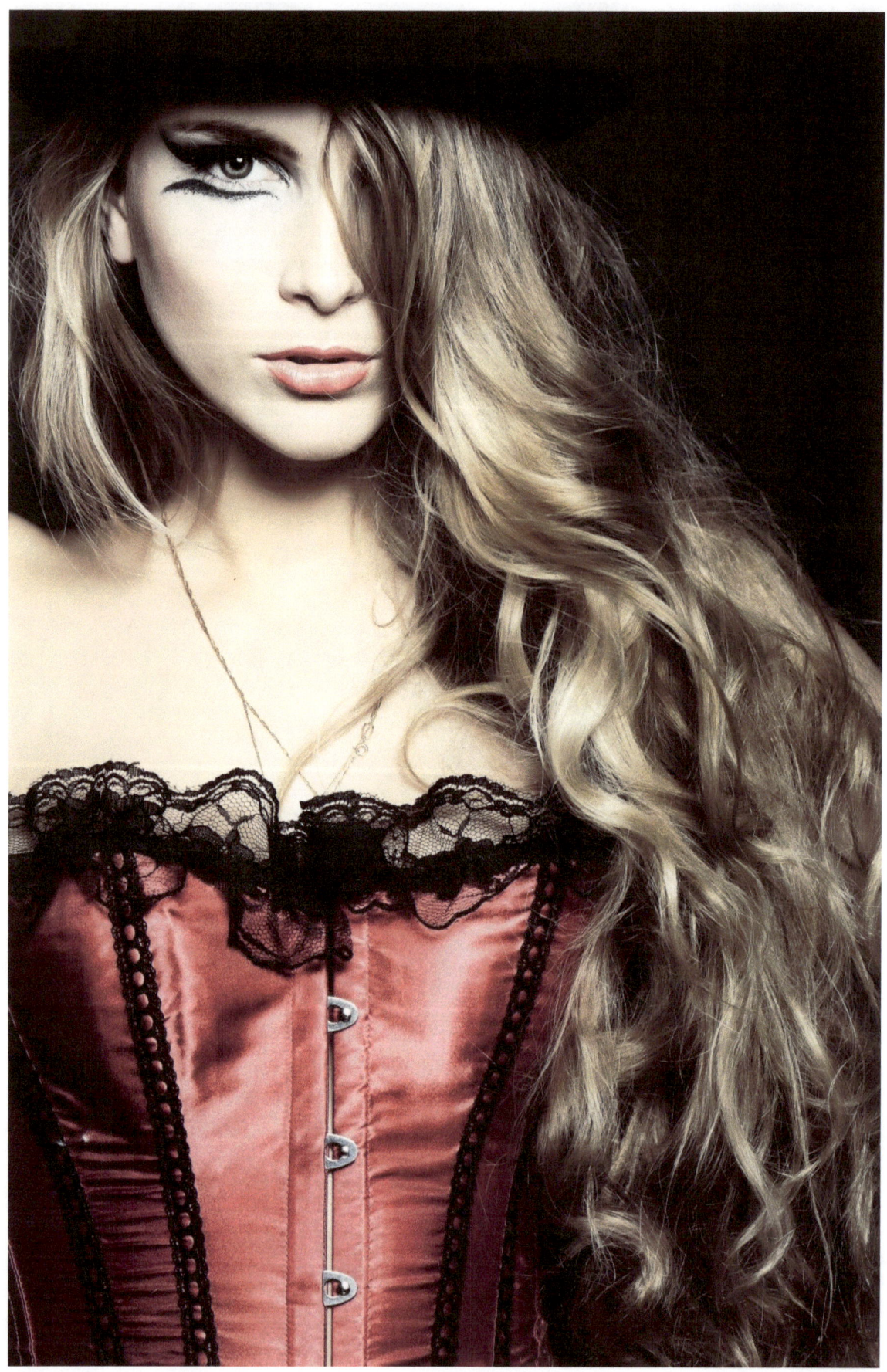

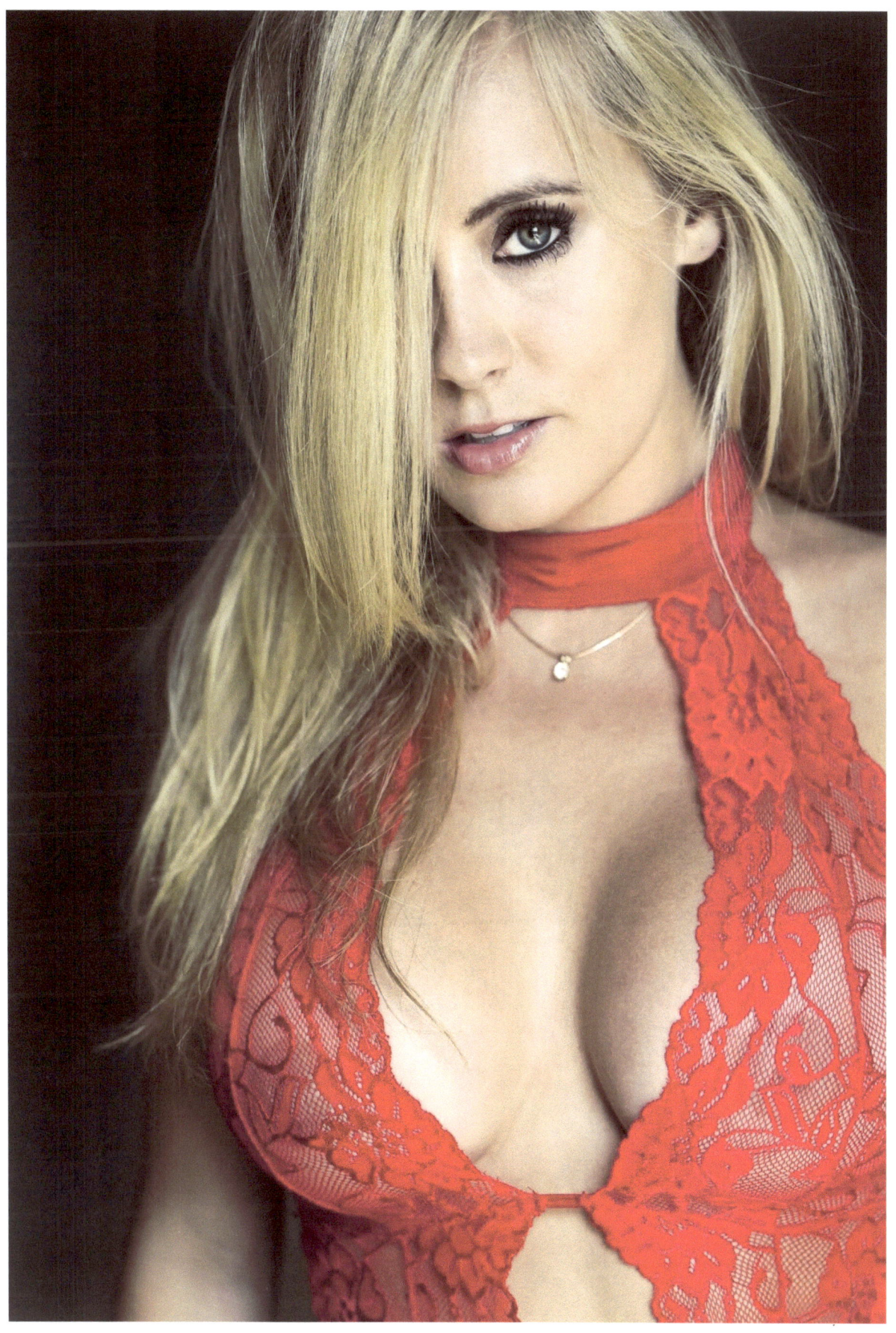

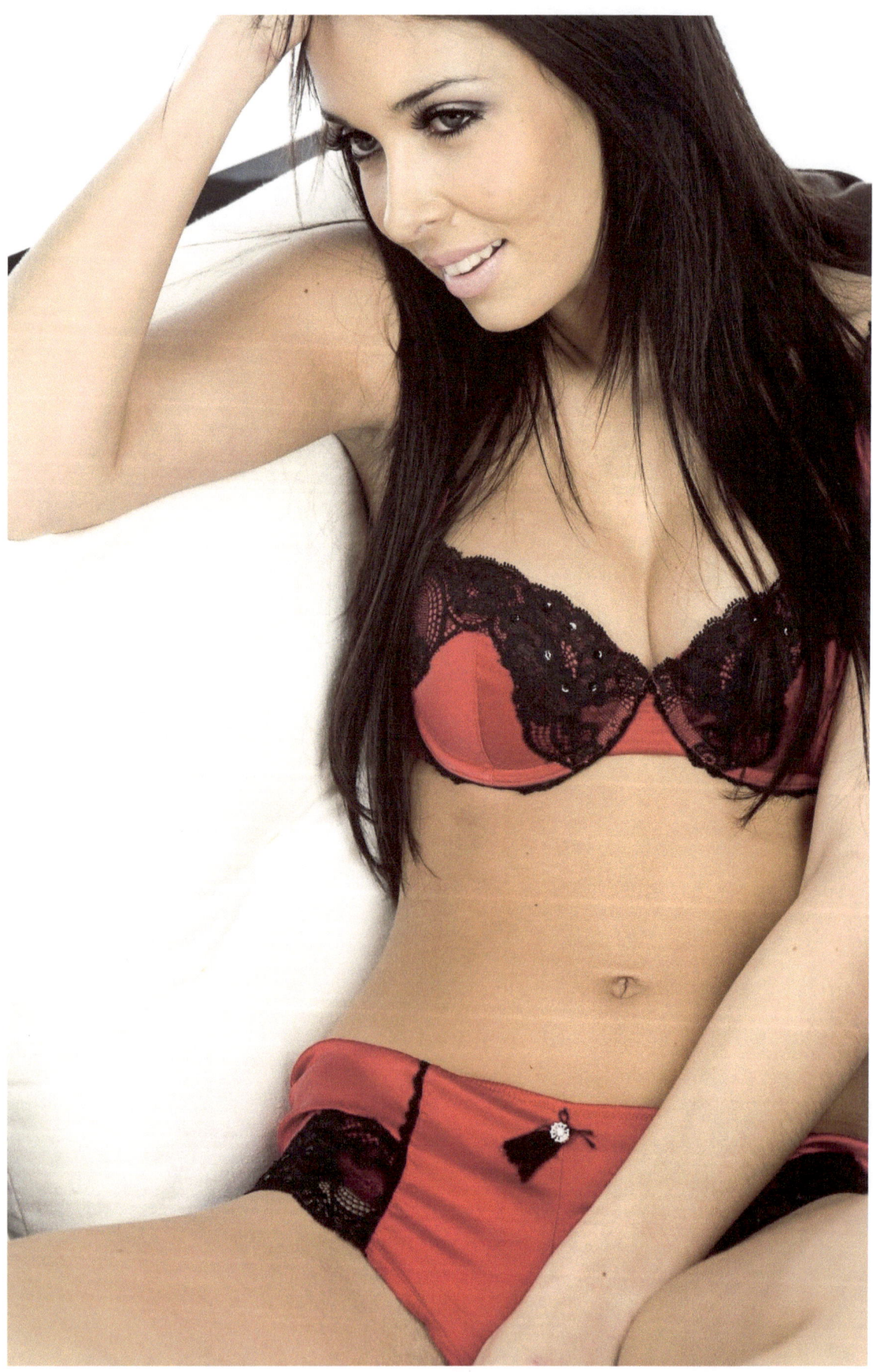

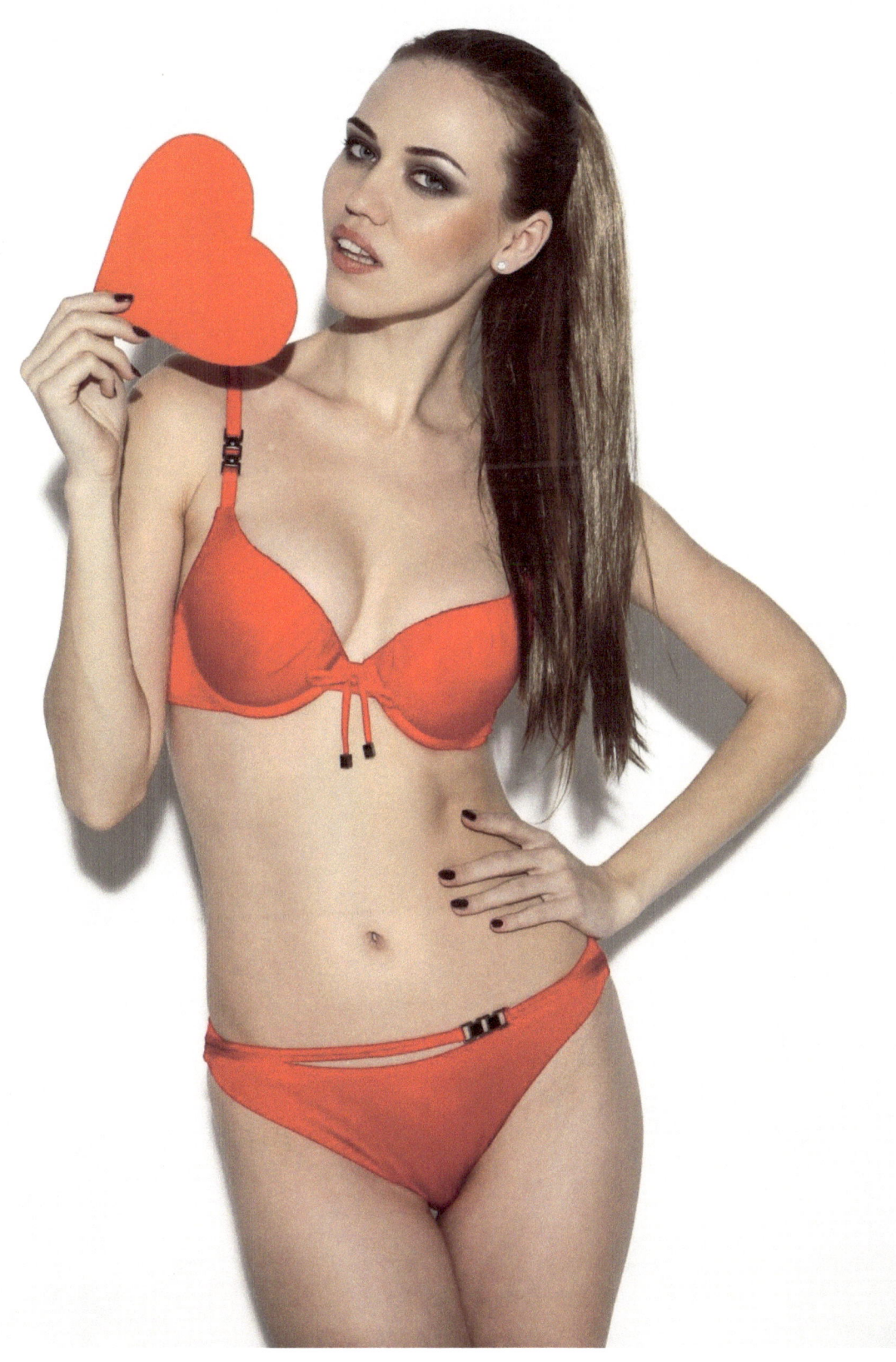

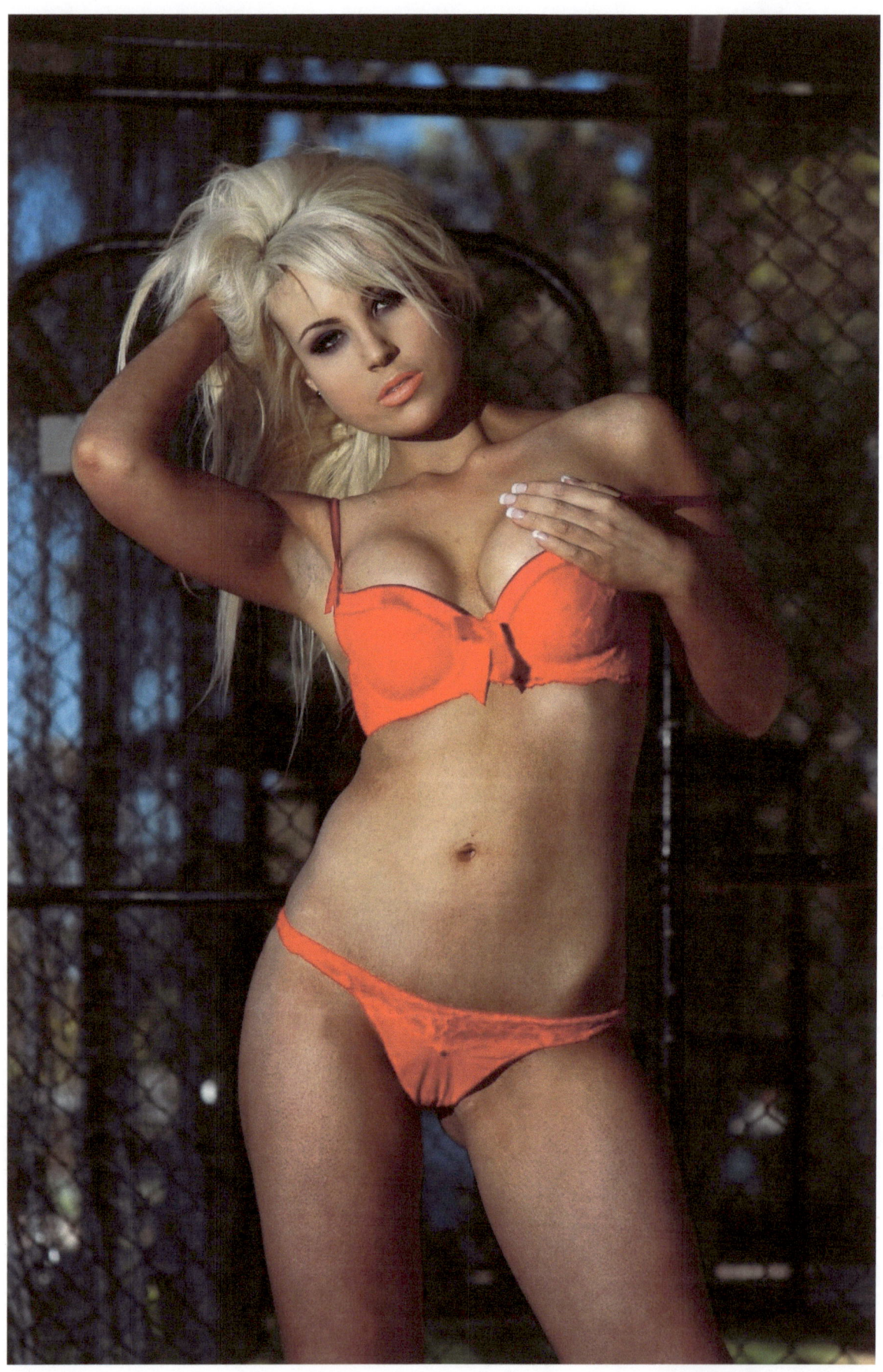

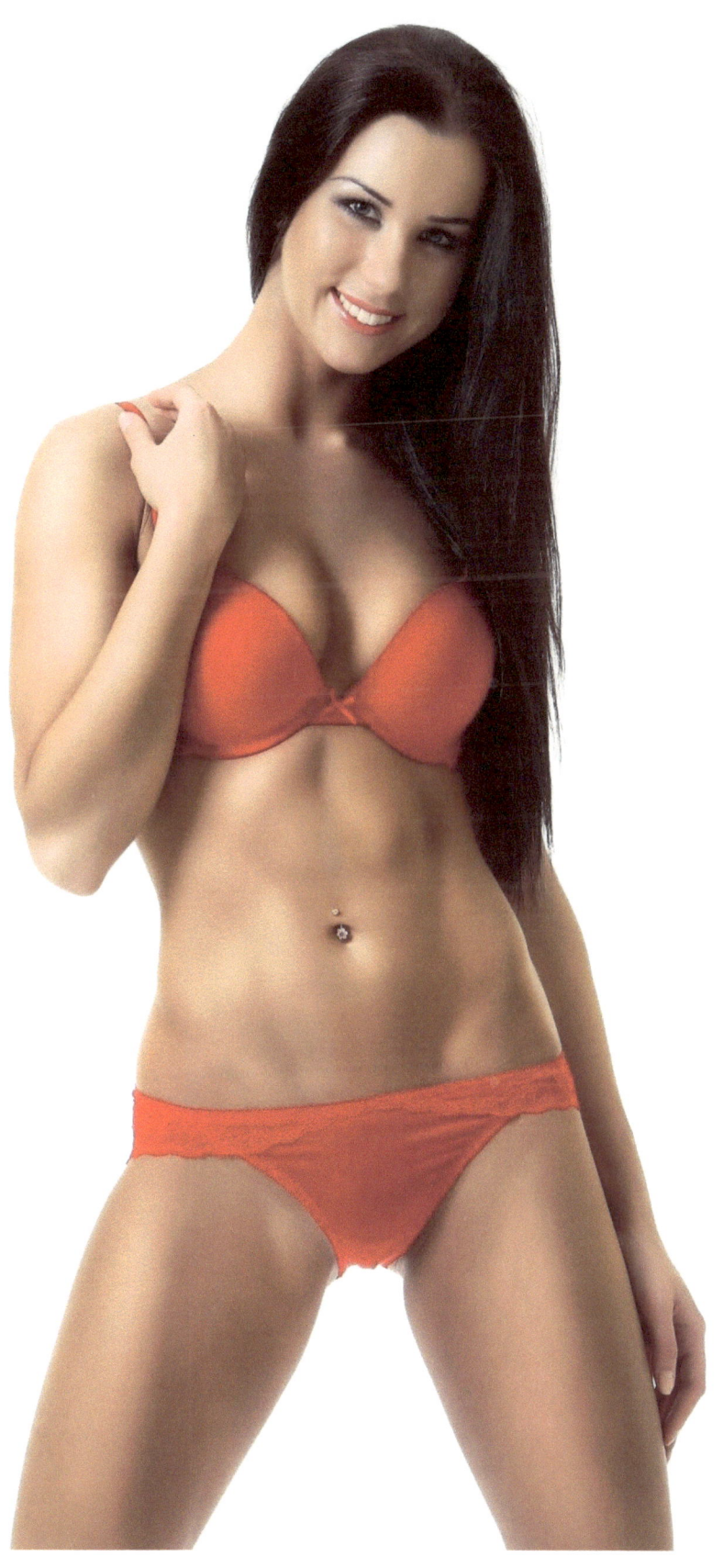

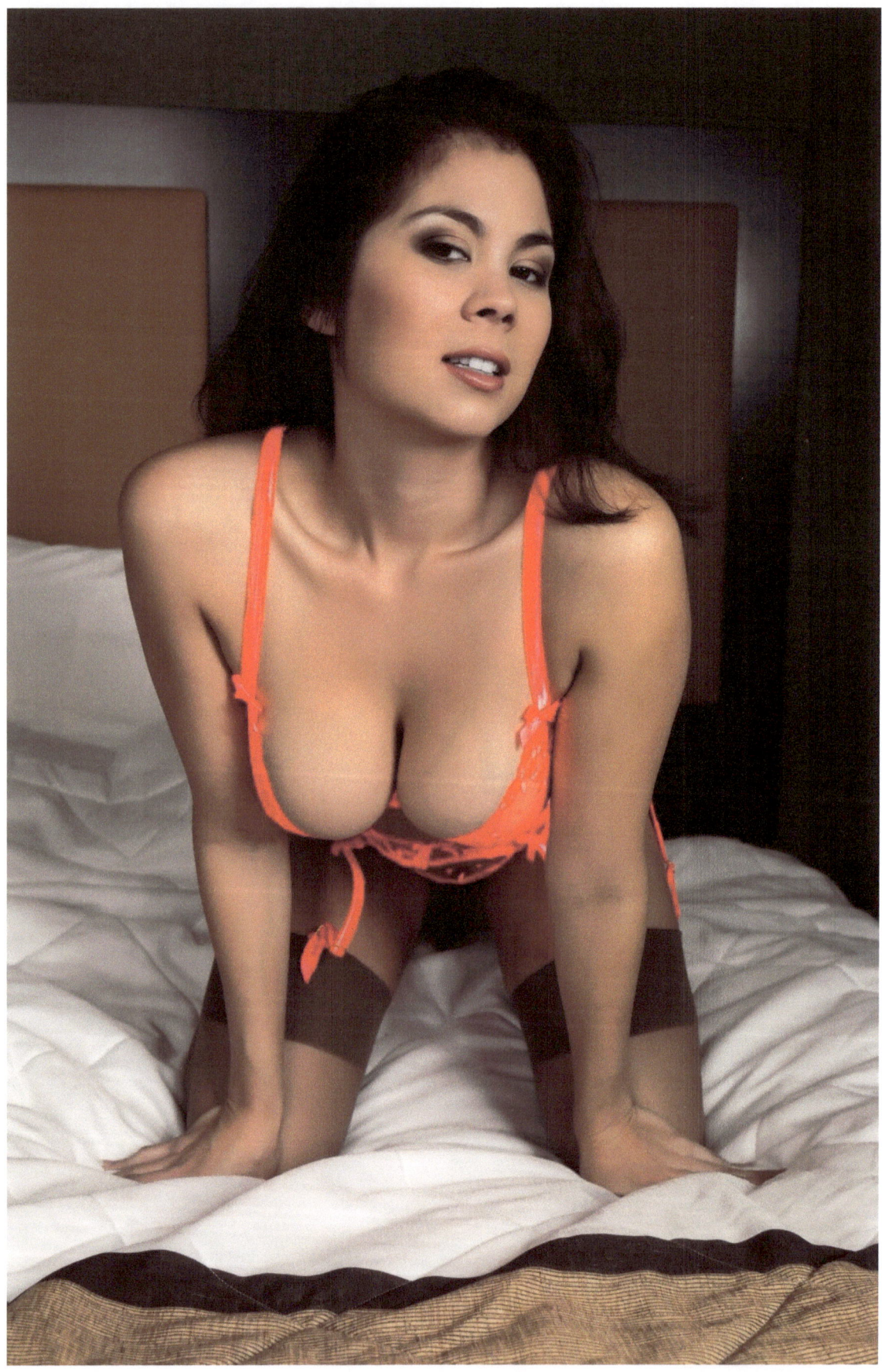

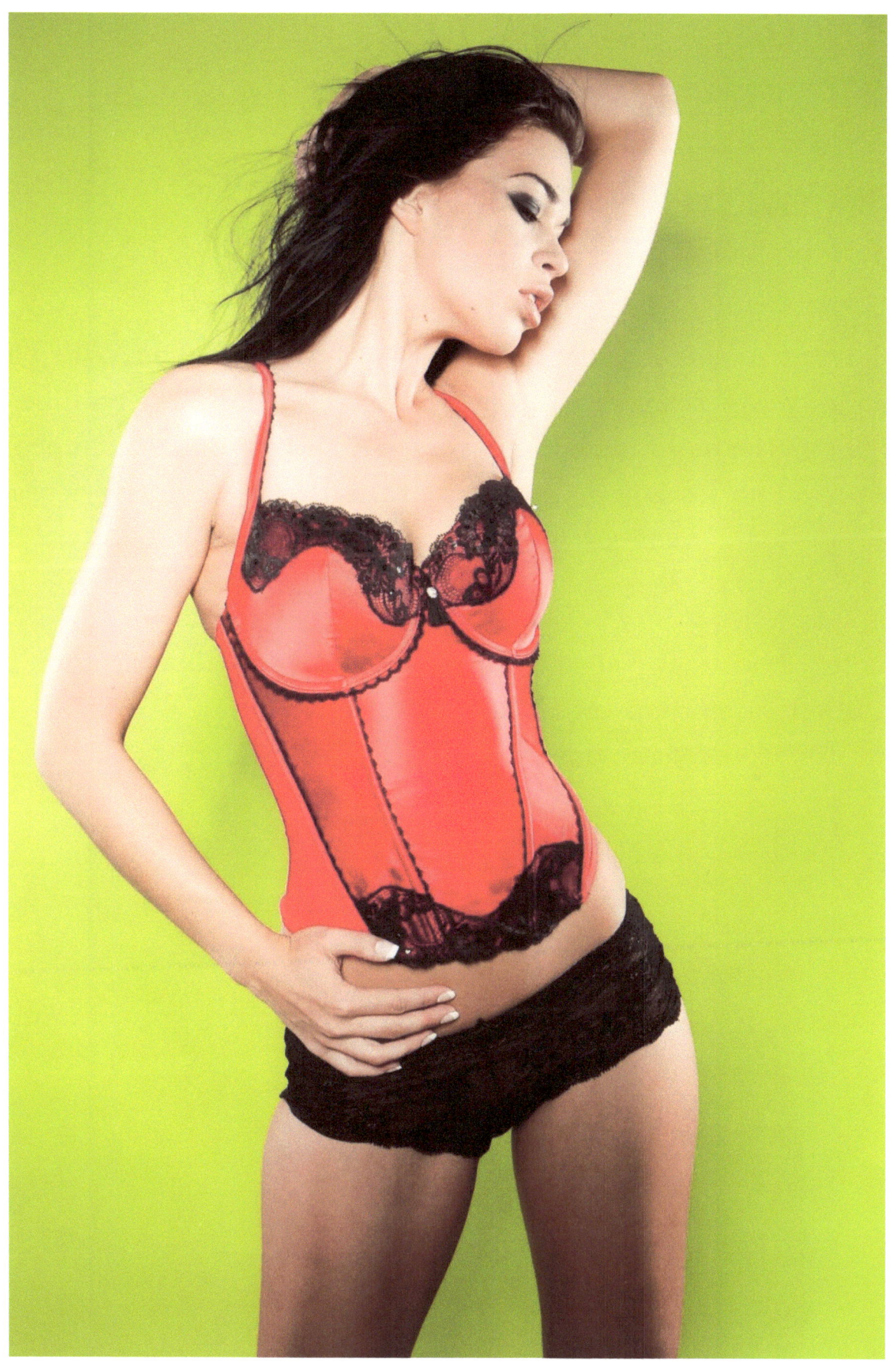

Compromising Positions

would like to thank you for your purchase and offer you the opportunity to join our members-only Facebook group.

Just post a screen-shot of your Amazon receipt to Anita Cocktail's Facebook wall at https://www.facebook.com/AnitaCocktail90 and you'll be invited to join in on the fun! Membership gets you sneak previews of upcoming books, first notice when a book is up for sale, and exclusive access to members-only pictures and stories.

We sincerely hope that you enjoyed these photos and hope that you'll take a look at other Compromising Positions titles by Anita Cocktail. Please do leave a review – we greatly appreciate it!